Original title:
Fables of the Fir Forest

Copyright © 2025 Creative Arts Management OÜ
All rights reserved.

Author: Elias Marchant
ISBN HARDBACK: 978-1-80567-353-8
ISBN PAPERBACK: 978-1-80567-652-2

Journey Through the Evergreen Veil

In a forest where trees play and sway,
Squirrels have parties by night and day.
A badger in boots dances on a log,
While frogs in tuxedos croak like a fog.

Wandering through tales that sprout and twist,
A chipmunk sings tunes that can't be missed.
The pines whisper secrets, giggles abound,
As laughter and whimsy echo around.

A Fox's Folktale

Once a fox with a hat so fine,
Tried to woo a duck with a bottle of wine.
The duck quacked, 'Dear sir, do take a seat,'
But the table was wobbly – oh what a feat!

With each clumsy step, he tripped on a root,
The duck rolled her eyes, then pecked at his suit.
The fox cried, 'Alas, my style's so chic!'
While the duck simply cackled, 'You're far from unique!'

The Dreaming Trees

Beneath a tree with a snoring bear,
A rabbit shares tales with a dragonfly pair.
They speak of the sun and dreams so absurd,
Like a cactus that sings and a talking bird.

Nearby, a raccoon stirs a pot of stew,
'This broth is so good, it's fit for two!'
Yet a skunk runs by, making all flee,
Proclaiming, 'Dinner's on me – whee!'

Beneath the Boughs of Time

Under branches where shadows dance and play,
A wise old owl naps the hours away.
A raccoon in pajamas reads tales by the light,
As a family of hedgehogs preps for a fright.

They whisper of ghosts dressed up like nuts,
Who dance and who joke and slide in their ruts.
The owl wakes up, gives a glance and a wink,
'Who knew the woods could be such a drink?'

The Sorrows of the Solitary Spruce

In a glade stood a spruce so tall,
With branches like arms that would gesture and sprawl.
He sighed to the creatures, "I'm lonely, you see,
Can't someone just hug me, or climb up with glee?"

The squirrels would chatter, too busy to care,
While the rabbits just giggled and hopped through the air.

The spruce rolled his eyes, and with a slight sway,
He whispered, "Next year, I'll just move far away!"

Eyes in the Underbrush

Beneath leafy canopies, shadows would roam,
Tiny eyes peek out, far away from their home.
A rabbit once called, "What's lurking out there?
Is it a friendly squirrel or a big monster bear?"

A voice from the bushes exclaimed, "I'm just shy!"
To which the wise owl croaked, "You're a mouse? Oh my!
The only true danger's a cat with a grin,
But I wouldn't take bets on 'who's likely to win.'"

The Chirp of Ancient Crickets

Old crickets with wisdom made music at night,
Their songs were a blend of the silly and bright.
"I once knew a beetle who danced on a leaf,
But stepped on a twig, oh, that was his grief!"

Another chimed in with a jump and a jig,
"Remember the ant who outgrew his own dig?
He strutted one day, like a star on a stage,
Till his pals in the ground wrote a book on his age!"

Chronicles of Woodland Creatures

In tales where the creatures all gather and meet,
There's laughter and antics, and antics are sweet.
The bear jokingly asked of a fox, "How's the chase?
I heard you got stuck in a tree with no space!"

The fox, with a smirk, said, "Not as stuck as you,
Last I saw you, you were lost in the dew!
But together we laugh, a great party awaits,
With news from the owls and a feast from the plates!"

Tales from the Timber Threshold

In the woods where the squirrels play,
A hedgehog danced, hip-hip-hooray!
He twirled and spun on tiny feet,
Said, "Who knew prickle could be so sweet?"

A rabbit pranked a wise old crow,
With a painted rock, a clever show.
The crow cawed loud, then rolled his eye,
"Next time I'll sit, not fly so high!"

A wise old tree taught fox to paint,
His art was wild, a little quaint.
The forest critters came to see,
Gasping at hues of blue and pea!

The chipmunk claimed he lost his stash,
But found it all with quite a splash.
In acorn caps, he held a feast,
"A nutty party, to say the least!"

The owl hooted tales of yore,
As animals gathered, craving more.
Laughter echoed through the glade,
For woodland friends, no need for shade!

The Enigma of the Elder Tree

Beneath the tree with bark so wise,
A squirrel crafted quite the disguise.
With leaves as clothes, he stole the show,
"I'm a tree!" he cried, "Just so you know!"

The rabbit asked, "Oh, what's the trick?
How come you never need a stick?"
The squirrel grinned, his nuts he'd stow,
"Fast fashion's key; I'm in the know!"

An owl perched high, the judge of fun,
Declared they'd race, just for a pun.
But as they ran, the elder sighed,
"Slow down, dear friends, enjoy the ride!"

As twilight fell, the stars came out,
The forest laughed, without a doubt.
With stories spun and dreams at play,
The dusk became the night's ballet.

Each creature's jest, a merry song,
In elder's shade, where all belong.
Embrace the quirks, let laughter reign,
For in this wood, joy's never plain!

Moonlit Musings of the Mossy Path

In the woods where the shadows dance,
The critters prance in a nightly trance.
A raccoon with a hat, oh what a sight,
He steals a snack under silver light.

The squirrels all chatter, tossing pine nuts,
While the owl hoots, and the fox struts.
"No acorns tonight, I'll take a chance!"
As the moon winks, they join the prance.

Mossy stones giggle, tickled by dew,
Fungi chuckles, reflecting the hue.
Beneath the stars, secrets unfold,
In this moonlit tale that never gets old.

And who could forget the deer with her flair?
Trying to dance, but ends up in the air.
With a tumble and a roll, she starts to laugh,
As the night spins on, like a fun photograph.

The Tale of the Timid Treetopper

High in the branches, a timid bird,
Hiding from shadows, he rarely stirred.
With a flutter and fluster, he'd peek around,
Hoping no trouble would ever be found.

The winds would tease, whispering low,
"Come out, little friend, put on a show!"
He'd waddle on limbs, a wee little frump,
Till a gust blew hard, giving him a jump.

Adventures await, if he'd just be brave,
But he twirled and tumbled like a wobbly wave.
With each little flop, his laughter rang clear,
"I might be a chicken, but oh, what a steer!"

And someday he'll soar, on wings made of cheer,
Dance with the clouds, without any fear.
For our timid treetopper, it's only a phase,
His funny escapades brighten our days.

Wandering Moss and Moonbeams

A mossy patch danced under the moon,
Whispering tales in a soft, leafy tune.
With giggles and glee, they began to sway,
As the moonbeams giggled, joining the play.

Patches of shade threw a friendly game,
"Catch us if you can!" they called out in fame.
But the deer came a-leaping, a bouncy delight,
Tripping on trinkets while chasing moonlight.

A hedgehog rolled by, all prickles and fun,
Mistaking the stars for bright little buns.
"Oh silly old friend," the owl said with a hoot,
"Just watch where you're going, or you'll end up a root!"

Yet laughter echoed through bark and through bough,
As wand'ring moss twinkled, and took a deep bow.
In the moon's soft embrace, they all finally lay,
Dreaming of mischief until the next play.

The Pine Spirit's Lament

In the heart of the forest, where the tall pines grow,
Lives a spirit who sighs, and puts on quite a show.
With branches a-quiver, and a moan like the breeze,
He's tickled by shadows dancing with ease.

"Oh what a job!" he groans with a grin,
"To guard all this beauty, where do I begin?"
While the squirrels conspire, and the raccoons tease,
He's stuck with his duties, a guardianship freeze.

But when night falls softly, with a wink and a glee,
He shakes up his needles, sets the creatures free.
A jig on the bark, a whirl among leaves,
With laughter that echoes, his heart believes.

So if you hear rustles while strolling the path,
Know it's the spirit, engaging in math.
Calculating joy, through jest and delight,
In the realm of the tall pines, under shimmering light.

The Guardian of the Grove

A squirrel in armor, standing so tall,
He shouts at the birds, declares, "No more squall!"
With acorns as weapons, he takes on the trees,
While raccoons giggle, whispering, "Please!"

The wise old owl gives a chuckle so deep,
As the guardian fumbles, starting to leap.
He trips on a root, sprawls down in dismay,
And the woodland critters just laugh all day.

Whimsy of the Woodland Spirits

Tiny fairies dance on toadstool rings,

With laughter so loud, it jigs all their wings.

They sprinkle their magic, giggling with glee,

As a mouse with a hat tries to sip herbal tea.

A raccoon in trousers steals shiny new spoons,

While foxes debate who can sing all the tunes.

The fun never ends in their merry parade,

As shadows and light twiddle through every glade.

Twilight Tales of the Thicket

When dusk starts to settle, the stories ignite,
With owls reading tales of the critters' delight.
A hedgehog, quite bold, tells of mischief and fun,
While bats mimic voices, swooping just for a run.

"Why did the rabbit cross over the road?"
The frog croaks the answer with just a slight goad.
"To hop on the jokes that the fox always tells!"
And the thicket erupts with melodious yells.

The Ghosts of Fallen Needles

In the nighttime mist, poke some ghosts in the air,

With laughter that echoes, and slight, playful flair.

They tell of old tales, each shadowy shape,

As pinecones watch on, dressed as tiny drapes.

A jester named Jack in his costume of green,

Springs out from the bushes, quite slick and quite keen.

He trips on a branch, yelps, "I'm just here to play!"

And the ghosts burst with giggles, gasping, "Okay!"

Reverie in the Rustling Leaves

In a forest where squirrels jest,
Chasing shadows, they never rest.
A rabbit wears a ridiculous hat,
While raccoons sing to a sleepy cat.

A wise old owl gives a knowing wink,
As acorns tumble, making them think.
The trees whisper secrets, all in jest,
While chipmunks boast about their best quest.

Beneath the boughs, laughter does grow,
As the brook giggles, putting on a show.
Frogs hop along with a splashy cheer,
Each ripple holds a ticklish sneer.

With a breeze that dances through each glade,
Nature's humor never seems to fade.
The forest thrives in playful delight,
With every critter in a comic fight.

The Howling Wind's Story

The wind loves to stir up a fuss,
Telling tales that make the tree trunks cuss.
It tickles the boughs, a mischievous sprite,
Swirling leaves into a dizzy flight.

Once it met a bear wearing a sock,
Who grumbled, 'Stop! You're both loud and shock!'
Yet the wind just howled, its voice like a song,
Saying, 'Join the fun, you can't feel wrong!'

Then a deer danced, with a hop and a twirl,
While the wind made her mane into a whirl.
Together they created a wacky parade,
Leaving behind a trail of charades.

Beneath the bright moon, they all found their groove,
With branches and creatures in a silly move.
The wind blew harder, a laugh in the night,
Making mischief and cheer till the morning light.

Whispers Among the Pines

In a realm where the tall pines lean,
Gossip flows like a bubbling stream.
The needles chuckle with every breeze,
Sharing secrets with the buzzing bees.

A turtle stumbles, wearing a shoe,
While squirrels admire him, 'What a view!'
The cicadas jive, buzzing in time,
Chirping along to a quirky rhyme.

Over by the brook, a frog takes a leap,
A tiny fish laughs from the shallow keep.
With a splash, he joins in the fun parade,
While the crickets play a jazzy serenade.

Through the laughter, the winds intertwine,
As the pines whisper tales of the divine.
Frogs, turtles, and critters galore,
In this woodland where giggles restore.

Shadows of the Evergreen

The evergreens stand, tall and proud,
Casting shadows that seem to crowd.
A raccoon juggling, what a sight!
As the sun dips low, into the night.

An acorn rolls, and a squirrel takes chase,
With a wobble and giggle, it's a comical race.
The owls hoot softly, sharing a laugh,
At the tumbling creatures on their silly path.

Beneath the branches, friendships bloom,
In this magical place where joy finds room.
A fox prances by, with a riddle to share,
While shadows play games, in the cool night air.

Laughter echoes through the darkened glen,
As starry skies twinkle again and again.
The evergreen's winks, a playful tease,
In the land where fun flows with the breeze.

Secrets of the Sylvan Glade

In a glade where squirrels play,
They gather nuts in their own way.
One dropped acorn, a funny sight,
It bounced around, then took a flight.

A rabbit danced with a jaunty hop,
While turtles strutted, thinking they're hip.
The foxes laughed 'til they fell down,
At the sight of a chicken with a tiny crown.

The wise old owl gave a knowing grin,
As the raccoons raced with their loot, full of sin.
But who stole the pie? Oh what a crime!
It was the badger; it happened all the time!

Lurking shadows in the soft twilight,
Brought forth tales, giggles, and delight.
For in this place where whispers spread,
Even the mushrooms dance in their bed.

Tales from the Timberland

In the timberland where tales unfold,
A porcupine once cursed the cold.
He put on a sweater, bright and pink,
Then laughed at the squirrels, said, "What do you think?"

A beaver's lodge began to sway,
As raccoons held a party, hip-hip-hooray!
With cake made of bark and a punch of pine,
They danced on the banks, oh how divine!

The chattering birds made quite the fuss,
About a lost hat and a raucous bus.
They flew in circles with feathers a-twirl,
As the fox tried to catch them, in a goofy whirl.

When the sun sets low, under the moon,
The creatures gather, all singing a tune.
With laughter that fades into night's gentle calm,
They share all their secrets, and joy like a balm.

Echoes of the Ancient Woods

In ancient woods where shadows drift,
The owls take bets on who's least swift.
A turtle challenged a hare to race,
And the bets were high, with laughter in place.

The trees let loose their giggly sighs,
As rabbits painted their backs like ties.
With tiny brushes, so carefully held,
They turned into art, a sight to behold!

A hedgehog found a pair of shoes,
And tried to tango, but sang the blues.
He tripped on his feet, and over he fell,
Creating a ruckus that rang like a bell.

When twilight blankets the woodlands grand,
The stories echo like a fun jazz band.
For every critter knows, with a wink and a cheer,
In the ancient woods, no place to fear!

The Canopy's Embrace

In the canopy high, where the branches twine,
A parrot squawked, "This tree is mine!"
With colors so loud, he stole the show,
While the critters rolled on the ground below.

The deer wore glasses, quite the sight,
Trying to read by the soft moonlight.
With a book open wide, upside-down too,
He asked the raccoon, "What's a 'moo'?"

An acorn dropped and startled a mouse,
Who rushed to escape, skittering about the house.
But the crow just cawed, "Try to stay calm!
It's just a small nut, not a scary bomb!"

So in the embrace of the rustling leaves,
With giggles and fun, the forest believes.
That laughter and joy are hidden in grace,
In the canopy's arms, it's the silliest place!

Pinecone Prophecies

A pinecone sat upon a throne,
Declaring wishes all alone.
With a twitch and shake, it made a sound,
"I decree! Pine nuts shall abound!"

The squirrels gathered round to cheer,
For hidden snacks that would come near.
But the cone just laughed, a prankster bold,
"I meant for you to share the gold!"

The wise old owl hooted in glee,
"A nutty jest, oh can't you see?"
As breezes danced with twinkling light,
They feasted well on fables bright.

Now every cone holds secrets sway,
With giggles tucked among the hay.
Those who listen, laughter will find,
In tales of trees and cheeky pine.

Resplendent Roots

Deep below, the roots did plot,
Planning mischief—what a lot!
They tangled vines and whispered lies,
Making flowers roll their eyes.

"Let's swap the colors, yellow to blue!"
A daisy gasped, "Oh, what's this? Who?"
The pansy giggled, "Count me in!"
As petals spun, chaos did begin.

The tulips blushed in shades of green,
A garden feast, such sights unseen!
With earthworms chuckling underground,
Harmony in humor's found.

Nature's pranksters, roots that play,
A giggle blooms from night to day.
For each odd shade and blend they make,
Ensures together, friends won't break.

Wanderings through Whispering Woods

In woods where whispers softly creep,
A rabbit laughed—"Hey, mind the leap!"
He tripped on roots, fell with a bounce,
The trees just swayed; they'd scoff and pounce.

A fox with flair joined in the game,
"Let's see who's foolish, we'll stake our claim!"
The leaves all rustled, giggles spread,
While one young squirrel hollered, "Head!"

Branches tangled with giggly vows,
While critters danced in tiny rows.
With every step, a tale would flip,
In light-hearted jests, they'd wildly trip.

As dusk descended, shadows grew long,
The woods sang sweetly their laughter song.
For every wanderer who'd joined the fray,
Left with a chuckle, in blissful play.

The Treetop Oracle

Above the world, where branches tangle,
The Oracle swings, a goofy angle.
"Come seekers, gather! I'll tell your fate!"
But he forgot to check the date!

So when the beavers asked for a clue,
He said, "Be bold! Wear purple shoes!"
With puzzled looks, they scurried away,
Only to trip, in joyful display.

A squirrel swung by, full of cheer,
"What's this? Your prophecies are quite queer!"
But the truth struck hard from high above,
In every giggle, they found their love.

With tricky riddles and twists so bright,
The Treetop Oracle sparked pure delight.
For even stars, though wise they seem,
Smile wide at every silly dream.

Whispers from the Willow's Heart

In the breeze the willows sway,
Whispering secrets, come what may.
A squirrel with shades, so cool and bright,
Spins tales of nuts by the moonlight.

Frogs croak jokes from the pond's edge,
While the rabbits make a bushy hedge.
With each giggle, the shadows dance,
In the forest, all take a chance.

The owls hoot puns from their high perch,
While the mice host a lunchtime church.
Grassy carpets, tickle our feet,
Amidst the laughter, life's a treat.

So when you tread where laughter lives,
Know each twig has a tale it gives.
In nature's humor, we find our part,
Joyfully echoing from willow's heart.

A Dance of Pollen and Time

In a whirl of pollen, bees do play,
Dancing around blooms in a sunny ballet.
The ants in suits, so dapper and fine,
March on a trail like it's a grand line.

Beetles spin tales upon a bright leaf,
Turning mischief into comic relief.
Breezes giggle as they tease the sun,
While butterflies flutter, oh what fun!

The daisies gossip, petals ablaze,
Claiming the spotlight in the golden rays.
They chuckle at shadows that flit and flee,
While tulips blush like they're sipping tea.

In a whirl of laughter, watch time spin,
Every moment a dance, where joy begins.
In nature's embrace, we twirl and shine,
A jubilant waltz—a dance of pollen and time.

Murmurs of the Mossy Floor

On the mossy floor, whispers arise,
From creatures unseen, oh what a surprise!
The hedgehogs chuckle at an old tree stump,
While mushrooms giggle at every small thump.

A bunny hops with a top hat, so spry,
Casting a spell as the fireflies fly.
The damp smell of earth sings a wild tune,
As the sun dips low, making room for the moon.

Crickets compose their night-time show,
With bass by the frogs puttin' on a glow.
Each leaf a note, in nature's grand choir,
As laughter weaves through the branches higher.

So tread softly where magic can soar,
For the mossy floor holds tales galore.
In every damp crack, humor does bloom,
With each tiny whisper, dispelling the gloom.

Engravings on the Forest Floor

Beneath the trees, a story untold,
Engravings on soil where the sunlight's gold.
Each footprint a giggle, a skipped little dance,
As critters take turns in a whimsical prance.

The pinecones scatter, like laughter in air,
While the squirrels giggle, without a care.
With branches above, they hold the line,
Creating a circus that's simply divine.

From twigs to stones, the forest's graffiti,
Draws quirky sketches, oh, what a pity!
For every bark has jokes to send,
In woodsy whispers, around every bend.

So let your heart soar on this playful plot,
Where laughter's engraved, and life's never caught.
Among the foliage, grab your own store,
Find treasures and giggles on the forest floor.

Whispers Beneath the Canopy

Beneath the leaves, the squirrels chat,
With acorns stacked, they sit and chat.
A raccoon sings in a tree with flair,
While chipmunks dance without a care.

The owl hoots jokes on a midnight show,
While rabbits hop, putting on a toe.
They giggle loud, in the moonlight's glow,
In this forest fun, what a frolic flow!

A porcupine tells tales with prickly wit,
As trees sway, and the shadows flit.
The laughter rolls through every branch,
In whispers soft, the creatures prance.

So come and join this merry band,
Where silly stories and games expand.
In the woods where humor reigns supreme,
Beneath the canopy, life's a dream.

Secrets of the Tall Pines

In tall pines, secrets twist and twine,
A bear in shades sips sweet pine wine.
With honey and jokes, he offers a snack,
"Try my treat, or I'll give you a whack!"

The clever fox wears a hat quite bold,
Telling tall tales of treasures untold.
"I found a gold shoe!" he claims with pride,
While raccoons giggle, their eyes open wide.

A deer in glasses reads from a scroll,
With riddles and puns that take a toll.
Each answer leads to another good laugh,
As humor flows down the woodland path.

The tall pines echo with hearty cheer,
Inviting all creatures to gather near.
In the shadows and light, joy intertwines,
Revealing the magic of those tall pines.

The Enchanted Grove

In the grove where mischief blooms,
A tree frog croaks with zany tunes.
With leaps and flips, he steals the show,
While mushrooms giggle, just row by row.

A gnome plays tricks on the mossy ground,
While fairies sprinkle laughter all around.
They dance on petals, a bright parade,
With silly capers that never fade.

The hedgehog spins tales of pies so sweet,
While the busy bees buzz a funny beat.
With honey drizzles and a laugh that roars,
It's a wholesome party amid the furs.

In the enchanted glide of playful glee,
Nature's jesters invite you to see.
Join the fun in the grove's embrace,
Where laughter, like sunlight, lights up the space.

Echoes of the Evergreen

Echoes ring in the evergreen shade,
Where every sound becomes a parade.
The birds play tricks with their mimic songs,
And squirrels giggle as they leap along.

The mischievous winds carry tales of fun,
Tickling the branches, a dance they've begun.
In whispers soft, the old trees jest,
Holding secrets of laughter at their best.

A wandering snail tells jokes so slow,
While chipmunks scatter, putting on a show.
The loggers' laughter fills the air,
As echoes of mischief bounce everywhere.

So wander deep where the pines stand tall,
Join in the mirth, the camaraderie of all.
In nature's embrace, let the chuckles flow,
In the echoes of evergreens, let joy grow.

Tales from the Old Growth

In the heart of the tall tree's sway,
Squirrels plot a nutty ballet.
A raccoon wears a hat just so,
Thinking he's the star of the show.

The owl sings a tune quite absurd,
While foxes dance without a word.
Each branch holds a giggle or two,
In a forest where laughter grew.

Bees buzz by with a ticklish hum,
While ants march, feeling quite numb.
"Who knew trees could be so comical?"
Ask the wise old bat in the holler.

Roots chuckle at mossy pranks,
While the pond reflects their thanks.
In this grove, every tale is a cheer,
Where the odd is routine and clear.

Splinters of Forgotten Wisdom

A woodpecker taps a rhythmic beat,
As branches gossip while squirrels eat.
Each splinter holds a story told,
Of mischief and laughter, brave and bold.

The hedgehog rolls, he thinks he's grand,
While a snail moves slow, not quite as planned.
"Faster!" yells the tortoise with glee,
"Catch me if you can, come see!"

A worm wiggles, full of chit-chat,
Sharing secrets beneath the mat.
"Did you hear about the pinecone charm?
A sprig of mischief, all safe from harm!"

Branches laugh 'til the sun goes down,
While a beaver dons a shiny crown.
In this world, wisdom's a playful tease,
Sprouting smiles on the breezy trees.

The Pinecone Herald

Gather 'round for the latest scoop!
The pinecone's tales make quite a group.
A squirrel's tiff over a stolen nut,
Leaves the forest in a happy rut.

"Did you see the bear in a tutu?"
Whispers the rabbit, his eyes so blue.
"Who'd have thought that bugs could dance?
Now we have bugs in a jiggy trance!"

The fox chimes in with a cheeky grin,
"I once wore a dress made of green tin!"
Laughs bubble up, sprouting like shoots,
In the kingdom of quirky animal hoots.

In each whisper, a chuckle unfolds,
The forest alive with tales retold.
Where the odd becomes normal, it's clear,
The pinecone herald brings joy near.

Chronicles of the Bursting Buds

Little buds giggle, eager to grow,
While the flowers strut with a colorful show.
"Are you ready for spring's grand debut?"
As blossoms chatter with morning dew.

A frisky raccoon in the thicket grins,
Hiding tricks with a cheeky spin.
The branches sway, whispering loud,
"Who will join the unfolding crowd?"

Buds burst open with stories to tell,
Of mishaps and pranks where laughter dwells.
They bloom with a pop, colors galore,
An orchestra of giggles from nature's core.

So, gather in spring's delightful spree,
In this forest of joy, wild and free.
With every petal and burst of green,
The chronicles unfold—oh, what a scene!

Legends of the Woodland Realm

In the realm where squirrels scheme,
A raccoon plots a silly dream.
He dresses up in a fancy hat,
Chasing shadows, here and there, fancy that!

The owls gossip late at night,
About the mice who started a flight.
With tiny wings and loud squeaks,
They soar in circles, oh what peaks!

Foxes play tricks on the bugs,
Swapping places with fuzzy rugs.
The grumpy old bear rolls his eyes,
At furries plotting their silly lies.

Bunnies dance in joyful glee,
Twirling round a knobby tree.
Laughter echoes around the glades,
In the crazy woodland charades!

Shadows Among the Spruce

Beneath the spruces, shadows crawl,
A1gaggle of critters having a ball.
A hedgehog juggles acorns with flair,
While a turtle giggles, caught in mid-air!

The chipmunks chirp a funny tune,
Moonlight dances with a cheeky raccoon.
They all prance under the laughing stars,
Playing tag with the night and its bizarre cars!

A beaver builds a wobbly den,
While squirrels argue, "Who's got the pen?"
Everyone falls in a heap of jest,
The spruce trees sway, they can't help but rest.

With shadows twirling in wild delight,
Forest creatures fondly unite.
In the brush, ghosts of fun take flight,
Under the watch of sparkly light!

The Tale of the Moonlit Trail

On the trail where the moonlit falls,
Listen closely, hear the mauls.
A fox with boots struts down so bold,
Claiming he's got a heart of gold!

The rabbits giggle, pointing with glee,
While sneaky geese scoff by the tree.
"Oh dear fox, you're too slick,"
"Why don't you try to dance a quick?"

The moon gave a nod, shone ever bright,
As the woodland held its breath with delight.
With a leap and a twirl, the fox took flight,
Spinning and hopping, oh what a sight!

But he tripped on a twig, oh what a mess,
He laughed so hard, he caused quite a stress.
The critters rejoiced in the sweet moon glow,
For the best trails lead where laughter flows!

Stories from the Thicket

In the thicket thick and lush,
Silly creatures make a rush.
The frogs wear ties, all smart and neat,
Chattin' about their tasty beet treat!

A wise old fox whispers a riddle,
While birds chirrup and wiggle a little.
"Why did the cow jump over the moon?"
"Because she heard it played a lovely tune!"

Porcupines gather for a grand feast,
With jam and bread, they're quite the beast.
But watch out for the tricky raccoon,
Stealing snacks, he's gone too soon!

As night creeps in, the stars take a peek,
"Tell us a tale," they all seem to seek.
In the thicket, laughter reigns bright,
Where absurd stories keep hearts light!

Legends Beneath the Fir Canopy

Beneath the sky, where shadows play,
A squirrel wore shades on a sunny day.
He danced around, all full of flair,
While a bird in a beak hat gave him a stare.

A wise old owl with spectacles round,
Told tales of nuts that were lost and found.
The trees would giggle, rustle in glee,
As the sun poured gold for all to see.

The rabbit took bets on who could hop high,
While the fox cracked jokes as he strolled by.
The laughter echoed from branch to root,
In this forest of fun, nothing was mute.

At dusk all critters began to chat,
Even the shy ones—oh, imagine that!
They shared their snacks and danced till night,
In this canopy of joy, everything felt right.

The Last Tree's Tale

In a clearing stood one lonely pine,
Whispering secrets over mugs of brine.
His branches swayed, a rhythmic dance,
To stories of squirrels and their wild prance.

A fox strolled in wearing a plaid shirt,
Claiming he'd traveled, oh, what a feat!
He packed up stories like it was a sport,
Of owls with hats and trees that snort.

Once a year, a bash they held,
With fruit punch brewed, the magic smelled.
They laughed, they twirled, spun round and round,
In the dirt, their tales brightly crowned.

So heed this tale from the last tall tree,
Where mirth and laughter flow endlessly.
For if you seek joy, just come on round,
You'll leave with memories forever unbound.

Spruce Sagas

In the shadows of spruce, a party's begun,
A raccoon DJ spinning tracks, oh what fun!
With nuts for snacks and cider brewed,
The woodland critters, all in a mood.

The chipmunks competed in acorn rolls,
While the deer did yoga to calm their souls.
Bubbles floated from a beaver's surprise,
As he stitched some vines, to no one's surprise!

A bear brought a grill, made burgers with glee,
While critters joined in for a sweet jamboree.
They sang and they laughed, the night wore on,
Under the stars till the break of dawn.

So if you wander near spruce and fir,
You might just hear a tale that'll stir.
For in the heart of this leafy spree,
Lies a rhythm of joy that sets them free.

Chants of the Charmed Grove

In a grove where whispers tickle the leaves,
Mice put on capes like natural thieves.
They planned a heist for the biggest cheese,
While frogs croaked tunes, aiming to please!

A dancing moose wore a tutu bright,
Twisting and turning, a hilarious sight.
The owls in the trees kept rigorous time,
As each finger tapped to a silly rhyme.

With fireflies glowing, the night came alive,
The woodland crew had learned to thrive.
In a raucous cheer, they'd sing and prance,
With the magic of laughter, they'd all take a chance.

So heed the calls from the charmed grove clear,
Where funny unfolds and all feel near.
In this circle of joy, friendships unfurl,
For laughter brings light to the forest swirl.

The Watcher of the Canopy

Up in the trees, where the squirrels play,
A watcher peers down, in a funny way.
With big round eyes and a grin so wide,
He chats with the birds, they can't help but hide.

A parrot flew in, all colorful and bright,
"What secrets do you see from such a height?"
"I see you stealing berries from the ground!"
Said the watcher with laughter, a joke so profound.

The owls would hoot, their wisdom bemused,
At the antics below, they often perused.
"A dance-off at dawn? I'm in for the fun!"
Said the watcher, as day brought the sun.

So up in the trees, they all throw a party,
With laughter and music, it's never too hearty.
In this leafy domain, they frolic and beam,
For the watcher and friends, it's a whimsical dream.

Beneath the Branches This Way Lies

Beneath the branches, a path full of cheer,
Where creatures concoct a delightful frontier.
A hedgehog named Fred, with a hat on his back,
Led the way forward down the leafy track.

"This way to fun!" he exclaimed with a grin,
"Where laughter and games are sure to begin."
A rabbit, so fast, zipped ahead with a cheer,
But tripped on a root, and then vanished, oh dear!

The tortoise named Tim, with a chuckle so deep,
Strolled on, never hurrying, never lost sleep.
"Join us, dear friends! Take a break from the race,
Here under the branches, there's always a place!"

So they danced in a circle, goofy and bright,
With a melody funny that rang through the night.
In this wooded wonder, beneath leafy skies,
The magic of friendship was no great surprise.

The Mischievous Mice of Maple Glen

In Maple Glen lived some mice with a plan,
To steal all the cheese, oh, they were a fan!
With tiny little feet and mischievous grins,
They plotted and schemed for their savory wins.

They snuck through the cracks, oh so very sly,
With whispers and giggles, they'd give it a try.
But one little mouse tripped and squeaked out a sound,
And the whole cheese stash came crashing down, oh how profound!

"Quick, grab a piece! Before the cat knows!"
They darted and dashed, like little heroes.
They danced 'round the crumbs, in a cheese-filled delight,

Making merry and music till the fall of the night.

Yet the cat pounced out, with eyes all aglow,
But the mice had a trick, oh, how they did show!
With a wink and a wiggle, they dashed through a hole,
Leaving the cat scratching, quite out of control!

Needle and Leaf: A Chronicle

In a forest so grand, where the green branches sway,
Lived Needle and Leaf, having fun every day.
With stories of mischief that echoed so loud,
They'd gather the critters, attracting a crowd.

"Did you hear, my friend, of the skunk with a hat?"
Said Needle with giggles, as Leaf bore some chat.
"He wore it all day, till the sun finally set,
Then tripped on his tail, oh, a sight you won't forget!"

With laughter contagious, the animals cried,
As Needle and Leaf spun more tales side by side.
"Remember the day that the crow tried to sing?
The tune was so funny, it made the trees swing!"

So they'd share silly tales, from slumber to dawn,
In the heart of the forest, where friendships are drawn.
With Needle and Leaf, every creature could see,
That fun and good cheer lived in harmony!

Spirits of the Mossy Path

In the woods where the pathways twist,
Ghostly giggles and jokes persist.
Mossy sprites with a glimmering grin,
Play hide and seek where no one had been.

They tickle the toes of each passerby,
Making them hop as they laugh and sigh.
Beneath the trees, they dance with glee,
Whispering pranks just for you and me.

Little goblins in caps and shoes,
Always ready to spread the news.
With each rustle of leaves, they weave,
A tale of laughter on this eve.

So venture forth and beware their charms,
For they may lead you to their arms.
With giggles echoing through the night,
The mossy spirits keep it light.

The Squirrel's Secret Cache

In a hollow tree where secrets lie,
A squirrel hides nuts, oh me, oh my!
With twinkling eyes, he stashes away,
Creating a feast for a winter's day.

His pals come by with a curious peek,
Oh, what treasures has he to seek?
Pinecones and acorns, a furry delight,
But he warns, "Keep it quiet, or we'll have a fight!"

One slip of a paw, and all nuts drop,
The critters scatter, a comical hop.
Chasing and tumbling, a nutty ballet,
The forest erupts in a playful fray.

With giggles and squeaks, they race to retrieve,
The lost little acorns, oh how they believe!
In the grand woodland, they'll always thrive,
Where laughter and nuts truly come alive.

Dance of the Leafy Guardians

Under the boughs with a crown of green,
Leafy guardians plot mischief unseen.
With rustling leaves and shimm'ring light,
They wiggle and giggle, a whimsical sight.

Twisting and twirling, a dance in the breeze,
They playfully tease the wandering trees.
"Catch us if you can!" they cheerfully call,
As branches bend low, trying not to fall.

From the ancient oaks to the sprightly birch,
Their leafy laughter begins to lurch.
A game of tag with the sunbeam's rays,
Spreading joy in a leafy maze.

So wander on through this playful grove,
Where the guardians waltz, and nothing's a trove.
Each rustle a chuckle, each shadow a grin,
In this leafy dance, let the fun begin!

Mysteries of the Timbered Heart

In the depths where shadows softly creep,
Timbered secrets, way too deep.
Trees that whisper tales of yore,
Of mischievous antics and woodland lore.

Knots and gnarls on an old oak's skin,
Sketches of laughter buried within.
A tale of a bear who tried ballet,
And a wise old owl's comedic display.

As night descends, the moon shines bright,
Creatures gather for the evening's light.
Jokes are exchanged, and stories grow tall,
In the heart of the woods, they all have a ball.

So listen closely, just take a seat,
For the timbered heart holds a rhythmic beat.
With every rustle, and every cheer,
Mysteries abound, bringing joy near.

The Winter's Whispering Spirits

In the chill of the night, the owls do hoot,
Squirrels in pajamas, a comical suit.
Snowflakes dance gently, like feathers they fall,
As the trees tell their tales, echoing their call.

The rabbits in boots, hop here and there,
Gossiping softly about winter's fair.
With a flick of their tails, they joke and they tease,
While the moon shines down, wrapping them with ease.

A hedgehog in glasses reads a tiny book,
Noses together, the creatures all look.
As they share silly stories around the pine,
Each laugh bursts like bubbles, sparkling and fine.

So come, heed the spirits of winter's delight,
Where giggles and whispers make everything bright.
In a patch of soft snow, the fun takes its course,
With the forest alive, every heart beats in force.

Lullabies of the Forest Floor

The crickets are chirping their nightly song,
While the mushrooms giggle, 'We've waited so long!'
With napping raccoons in a cozy array,
The forest's alive in a snuggly ballet.

A hedgehog hums softly, nestled in leaves,
Telling the fairies, 'I'll help you with thieves.'
But the shadows just chuckle at their busy plight,
For the stars above wink at the charming sight.

The fox in the clearing does a little jig,
While the frogs start to croak, oh so big!
Li'l bugs gather close for a dazzling show,
As the laughter of the night begins to flow.

In a world made of dreams, where silliness reigns,
Every creature joins in, shaking off pains.
With lullabies whispered, the forest will sway,
As the moon smiles down on the magical play.

Guardians of the Green Canopy

Beneath leafy arches, the chatter is grand,
Trees take to gossip, creating a band.
With sycamore strumming on branches so wide,
While the willow sways softly, with laughter as guide.

The raccoons in masks stage a midnight show,
Twirling and spinning, stealing the glow.
'How many acorns did we stash last week?'
The squirrels retort, 'Only the ones that squeak!'

A wise old owl hoots with a chuckle so deep,
His wisdom makes all of the forest creatures leap.
As the clouds drift along, sharing ticklish breeze,
The guardians laugh loudly, with utmost ease.

In the underbrush' shade, mischief unfolds,
With secrets and whispers, the humor it molds.
Together they dance 'neath the shimmering light,
The keepers of joy, till the end of the night.

The Conifer's Quietude

In the still of the pines, where the silence sings,
A raccoon dons slippers and handles the strings.
The pinecones are clapping, the branches are swaying,
While the forest stands still, in laughter, relaying.

A squirrel spills syrup on pancakes so round,
With bees all buzzing, making merry sound.
Each creature has stories, both silly and true,
Where the air is thick with a playful view.

A timid old tortoise challenges the air,
Declaring, 'I'm faster if you really dare!'
The rabbits giggle at his slow-moving pace,
In this quietude, joy finds its right place.

With laughter and whispers, the moments will last,
In the embrace of the trees, where the fun is amassed.
And when the sun sets, their spirits shoot high,
In the conifer's arms, they share a soft sigh.

Harmonies of the Hollow

In the hollow, a squirrel sings,
With nuts tucked tight under soft wings,
A rabbit joins with a hop and a cheer,
While a snail hums softly, without any fear.

The owl spins tales of the night's giggles,
While fireflies dance and flash like wiggles,
A chorus of critters, all in a row,
Sharing wild stories of ages ago.

The hedgehog jokes in a prickly style,
And the fox ruffles leaves with a playful smile,
They chuckle at shadows that leap and prance,
In this joyful forest, they all love to dance.

When dawn approaches, the laughter won't cease,
For in this hollow, there's never a piece
Of silence too long, it's a vibrant spree,
With melodies woven from nature's decree.

The Oak's Secret Confession

Underneath the old oak's wide brim,
A wise raccoon starts to spin a whim,
He tells of a time it lost its grand hat,
And how a crow stole it to sat on a mat.

The branches whisper tales of the sky,
While squirrel giggles, with a twinkle in eye,
"Oh dear old oak, you look quite absurd,
With birds in your crown, and leave's gentle word!"

The oak rolls its rings, a leafy delight,
Confessing how squirrels can't fly, what a sight!
While below, a rabbit just shakes its head,
At the antics of friends who just can't be bred.

And as the sun sets, a giggle escapes,
From critters who dance in their last little capes,
For in the old oak, secrets are spry,
And laughter lingers where shadows can lie.

Myths of the Misty Thicket

In the thicket where shadows play bold,
A turtle claims to be terribly old,
While the bunnies tease and twirl around,
What myths they weave in the green, lush ground.

A chameleon hides in a cloak of green,
Whispering legends of things that he's seen,
While frogs croak songs of the stars and the tides,
All while the hedgehog giggles and hides.

A spider spins threads of tales quite grand,
Of a dragon that danced on a magical land,
The fox rolls around, full of silly hope,
Claiming none of it's true, but dreams are just dope!

As night covers thicket in soft, velvet shrouds,
The laughter still echoes, of nature's proud crowds,
For while myths might be silly under moon's silver beams,
They craft all the colors of our wildest dreams.

The Lullaby of the Leafy Realm

In the leafy realm where the breezes play,
A raccoon strums on its banjo all day,
With melodies soft that tickle the trees,
While the owls give hoots in a jazzy breeze.

The critters gather, under the moon,
To sway to the rhythm, all in good tune,
A porcupine twirls with a quill-some jig,
While a badger bumps up with a funny little dig.

From branches above, a wise turtle declares,
"Life's a grand party, so let down your hairs!"
They laugh and they frolic, till stars do appear,
And the lullaby soothes every tiny ear.

As night blankets leaves in glorious hues,
The woodland hums softly, a sweet-hearted muse,
For in this lush haven, joy is the theme,
Spun by the leaves in a whimsical dream.

Harmony of the Woodland Creatures

In a glade where the critters play,
The squirrel dances in a wacky way.
The rabbit hops with some funny flair,
While the deer just prances without a care.

The fox tells tales with a cheeky grin,
As the hedgehog spins, they all join in.
The birds are chirping in gleeful cheer,
Making woodland melodies we all hold dear.

But oh! A raccoon steals the snacks in flight,
Creating chaos in the morning light.
The laughter echoes, the fun won't cease,
In this woodland party, there's joy and peace.

So if you're lost and seeking delight,
Just follow the sounds, both merry and bright.
For in this realm where creatures combine,
The harmony thrives, and all is divine.

The Lament of the Lost Acorn

Oh, little acorn, where could you be?
I left you here, beneath the old tree.
A squirrel laughed as he ventured away,
Now I'm left to ponder this gloomy day.

I searched high and low, behind every rock,
Past the babbling brook where the frogs love to croc.
The chipmunks chuckled, they thought it was grand,
While I paced around, feeling quite bland.

In the end, I found a nutty friend,
Who shared his treasure, a joyful amend.
We clinked our acorns, gave a shout of glee,
Turns out I lost it, but gained a spree!

So here's to the journey, the twist and the turns,
From searching alone, to new friends who learn.
Sometimes a loss can bring sweet delight,
In the laughter of all, every wrong feels right.

The Owl's Midnight Rhyme

Atop a branch, a wise old owl,
Sings a tune that makes the night prowl.
With a hoot and a wink, he starts his show,
All the creatures below start to glow.

The raccoons clap with their tiny paws,
While the rabbits wiggle and wiggle their jaws.
The possum hangs, playing maracas by ear,
There's laughter and music, a wild frontier.

He weaves a tale of the moonlit skies,
Of wormy snacks and surprise midnight fries.
The stars start twinkling, joining along,
In this crazy concert where everyone's strong.

So if you hear an owl in the night,
Join the party, it'll feel just right.
For in the woods, where the laughter climbs,
Magic awaits in the sweet midnight rhymes.

The Song of the River Stone

There's a stone by the river, all slick and round,
Who dreams of adventures where fun can be found.
He's seen the fish jump, and the frogs have a race,
But he just sits still, with a sad little face.

One day a turtle came plodding his way,
And said, 'Hey there, Stone, let's roll out and play!'
So they slid down the bank, into quite a mess,
Creating their splash, they sure felt the stress.

They bumped into bubbles, the fish gave a cheer,
The stone couldn't believe it, they'd shifted a gear.
They giggled and grinned, sang tunes like a dream,
The river was dancing, alive with a gleam.

Now the stone tells the tale of his joyous new friend,
Of laughs and of splashes, this wasn't the end.
Sometimes stillness can hold the best lift,
Just roll with the flow, it's a marvelous gift.

Mythos of the Murmuring Leaves

Once a squirrel with quite the eye,
Thought he could fly and kissed the sky.
He leaped from a branch on a daring spree,
Landed in a pile of soft, green tea.

The whispers of leaves gathered about,
Chortling and giggling, laughing out loud.
"Next time, dear chap, try a safer way!"
But the squirrel just shrugged and tried for a sway.

A wise old owl perched high and tight,
Shook his head at the squirrel's silly flight.
"If only he'd heed the tales we've spun,
But oh, what a joy to watch him have fun!"

Branches would chuckle at antics displayed,
As creatures would gather, quite unafraid.
In the woods where the laughter flows free,
Life's silly adventures become mystery.

The Painting of Shadows Beneath Trees

The shadows beneath the grand old oak,
Paint silly figures, just like a joke.
A rabbit in top hat, a fox with a grin,
Hosting a tea party for all that come in.

The breeze carries jokes, tickling the leaves,
While critters disguise in their fanciest weaves.
A hedgehog in glasses reads tales of the night,
As all of the forest yields to delight.

A mouse on a podium sings off key,
And the buzzards all clap, quite happily.
"Who knew the woods held such talent so rare?
Let's keep the performance; we need more flair!"

Each evening the shadows dance and collide,
With laughter resounding where secrets reside.
Echoes of joy weave through branches above,
In the heart of the forest, a tapestry of love.

Enigmas of the Emerald Enclave

In a nook of the woods where the secrets are kept,
A raccoon named Charlie just sighed as he slept.
He dreamed of a pie that was big as a tree,
Awoke with a start, 'Oh, where is it, me?'

He summoned his pals, a deer and a crow,
"Let's search for the pie—come on, let's go!"
Through bramble and thicket they stumbled and tripped,
An adventure for snacks, oh how they had zipped!

They interrogated leaves, who whispered in rhyme,
And pondered with chuckles that time's not a crime.
But all they discovered were crumbs in the grass,
"For pie in the forest, we really must pass!"

Yet laughter erupted with each crazy blunder,
As they found bits of cake, not pie, what a wonder!
In life's little quests, it's always a treat,
For friendship and fun can't be beat in their fleet.

The Timber Merchant's Prayers

A timber merchant, sharp as a tack,
Prayed to the trees, "Don't give me no flack!"
He danced in the forest with an ax in his hand,
But the trees just chuckled, they'd made a grand stand.

"Oh please, dear trees, don't hide from the light,
My business relies on your growth, what a plight!"
The birches swayed softly, their bark full of glee,
"We'd never surrender; we love wild and free!"

He begged for some mercy, with humorous flair,
"Just one little branch, I can't grow a hair!
Let's make a deal, I'll spare you today,
If you give me a log—and then run away!"

The timber trees laughed, their laughter a sound,
As the merchant danced off with nothing around.
For nature's rich bounty gives life a sweet twist,
And in every soft whisper, no tree can resist.

Hues of the Hidden Haven

In a nook where colors dance,
A squirrel wore a tiny pants.
He laughed as he pranced on a log,
Chasing the tail of a chatty frog.

Trees twirled in raspberry hues,
As bees donned their finest shoes.
A raccoon juggled acorns with flair,
While chipmunks played tag without a care.

The sun peeked through with a smile,
As laughter echoed for a while.
In this bright patch, the fun was plenty,
With silliness a generous entry!

Every shade told a jesting tale,
Of foxes with hats, and owls with pails.
In this hidden haven so absurd,
Nature's giggles were clearly heard.

Foxfire in the Forest

Amidst the boughs where shadows play,
A fox told stories in a funky way.
With glow-in-the-dark fur and a wink,
He giggled softly, leaving you to think.

"Why did the squirrel cross the road?"
"To teach the chicken how to unload!"
His voice rang out like a merry song,
While butterflies danced, all day long.

Mice whipped cream pies at the tall pine,
For dessert was a prank and a grand design.
The owl hooted, "What on earth?"
As laughter erupted, bursting with mirth.

In the foxfire glow of the bright night,
Gags and giggles flew like stars in flight.
Each critter joined the raucous spree,
In a forest where joy was wild and free!

The Radiant Realm of the Ravens

In a realm where the ravens jest,
They cawed and cawed, never at rest.
With shadows swooping, they played their game,
Pretending to steal all the woodland fame.

Riddles flew from beak to beak,
"Who's the fairest? Let's take a peek!"
Cards were dealt with a flourish so bold,
And tales of treasure shared and retold.

They'd mingle with badgers, dapper and sly,
Who wore monocles and let out a sigh.
"Did you hear about the clever raccoon?
He tried to out-dance the light of the moon!"

Laughter erupted in raucous sound,
As the woodland buzzed, merriment found.
In this radiant realm, jokes took their flight,
As the ravens spread cheer under the moonlight.

The Silent Council of the Trees

In a grove where whispers met the breeze,
The trees held a council with utmost ease.
"Why did the pine think he was so wise?"
"Because he stood tall and touched the skies!"

The birch chuckled, her bark sleek and white,
"Spouting wisdom? That's quite a sight!"
While willows swayed with a slow, soft grin,
"Let's hear what the old oak has to spin!"

But the oak just snored, deep in his dreams,
While critters plotted and hatched their schemes.
Squirrels pirouetted on branches with glee,
Creating a ruckus in the marquee tree.

With laughter that bubbled like spring's first thaw,
The trees giggled silently, filled with awe.
In their stillness, they knew all was well,
For even the tall ones could joke and jell!

The Heartbeat of the Great Cedar

In the forest, a cedar stands tall,
With a heart so loud, you can hear it call.
Squirrels are dancing, quite out of tune,
While rabbits hop by, singing to the moon.

Branches wave gossip, like leaves in the breeze,
"Did you see that raccoon? He thinks he's a tease!"
The old owl chuckles, wise and chubby,
"Those stories they spin, are just plain scrubbly!"

The wind plays the flute, notes flutter and glide,
While pinecones roll by, holding giggles inside.
A bear swings his paws, trying to dance,
But trips over roots, no second chance!

So in this great wood, life's full of cheer,
Where laughter's as sweet as the song of a deer.
When the cedar's heartbeat makes all things sway,
You'll find joy in the forest, come laugh and play!

The Forest's Forgotten Fairytales

Once a snail dreamt of racing so fast,
He challenged the hare, "I'll win!" he laughed.
But with a huge shrug and a yawn so wide,
The hare simply slept, while the snail slimed by!

In the shadows, a sprite named Gill,
Tried to give a tree a very big thrill.
She tied it a bow, all bright and pink,
But the tree just sighed, "I can't be your link!"

The silly old fox, with a hat too tight,
Tried to impress birds that took flight at night.
"Look at my style!" he exclaimed with glee,
But tripped on his tail, oh dear, oh me!

When moonlight descends and the stars gleam bright,
The forest remembers its tales each night.
With giggles and grins, they all can be found,
In whispers of leaves, where laughter's unbound!

Rhythms of the Rooted Ones

Under the earth where secrets reside,
The roots tell tales with a wriggling pride.
"Did you hear of the mushroom, bold and round?
He thinks he's a king, of this soil-bound ground!"

A dance of the daisies, swaying with glee,
Joining the ants, small as can be.
The beetles applaud, with a grumble and roll,
While worms do a wiggly, rhythmic goal!

A fox with a flute, played a tune all day,
While trees softly hummed, in their leafy way.
"Join us!" they beckoned, "In this rooty fest,
Where laughter is deeper than the ground's soft rest!"

As twilight appears, with twinkles above,
The forest's heart dances, in a rhythm of love.
The rooted ones chuckle, as shadows blend,
In a merry old forest, where good times won't end!

Quest of the Curious Chipmunk

Once a chipmunk found, a map so grand,
It promised treasures, hidden in the sand.
He gathered his friends, all eager to see,
What wonders awaited, beneath the old tree!

With a leap and a bound, off they all sped,
While a sleepy old tortoise shook his thick head.
"The treasure you seek, it's not what you think,
It might be just nuts, or a berry, I wink!"

Through bushes and brambles, they found lots of cheer,
But the map led them straight to a picnic near!
"Popcorn and peanuts! This quest's quite a win!"
The chipmunk laughed loud, as they dove right in!

So lessons were learned; treasures don't fade,
In friendships and fun, these moments, they made.
As the sun set low, they shared stories of munch,
In the heart of their forest, a glorious lunch!

Dances of the Deep Forest

The mushrooms twirl in silly glee,
As the rabbit hops with a cup of tea.
Crickets play a wicked tune,
Underneath the bright, round moon.

Squirrels spin with acorn hats,
While parading with the chitchat rats.
Their antics leave the trees aglow,
In this fest where giggles flow.

Woodpeckers join, they're tapping beats,
As chipmunks shuffle on tiny feets.
The owls hoot with laughter loud,
Proudly watching their quirky crowd.

When morning dawns, the dance will end,
But memories of fun the forest will send.
For in every nook, every wildlife den,
There's laughter waiting to start again.

The Serpent of the Cedar

A snake with a hat, what a sight to see,
Gliding through branches, oh so carefree.
He tells jokes to the woodpecker's drill,
As the sun shines bright, and the world stands still.

"Why did the tree go to school?" he quips,
"To improve its roots and grow better tips!"
The birds burst out with raucous laughter,
As the serpent slithers, moving faster.

He boasts of a dance, oh so refined,
A twist and a twirl, utterly unlined.
The forest chuckles at his playful charm,
A sneaky grin, but never a harm.

At twilight's call, he settles down,
With tales to share of the humor around.
In the heart of the woods, he takes a rest,
For tomorrow brings more jokes, oh yes!

Stories in the Swaying Pines

The pines whisper secrets in the wind,
Of raccoons in masks and the mischief they pinned.
A tale of a bear, who danced on a log,
And lost his cool hat to a cheeky dog.

The squirrels all gather, their eyes wide with glee,
As the beaver adds spice with a splash of brie.
"And then," he says, with a flick of his tail,
"He tripped on a root, and he danced without fail!"

The wise old owl lends an ear so staid,
Though he has heard much of the foolish charade.
With a wink of his eye, he adds his own spin,
Hooting aloud, "Though you can't always win!"

In the land of the pines, every story can twine,
Where laughter and joy through the branches entwine.
With each little yarn, the forest wakes bright,
In a world full of fun and sheer delight.

The Fox and the Fir

A fox wore a scarf, quite snug and neat,
He pranced past a fir with remarkable feet.
"What's the latest gossip in your shady grove?"
The fir just chuckled, "Oh, there's much to wove!"

"The hare lost a race, and the crow got cold,
The turtles are plotting, or so I'm told!"
With a flick of his tail, the fox laughed anew,
"Let's gather our friends and start a barbecue!"

They called up the deer and invited the hare,
With a feast set under the sky, so rare.
As animals danced and laughter rang clear,
They celebrated life with nothing to fear.

As twilight fell and the stars popped bright,
The fox grinned wider, feeling just right.
In the heart of the woods, friendships would stay,
For every fox and fir, there's magic in play!

www.ingramcontent.com/pod-product-compliance
Lightning Source LLC
Chambersburg PA
CBHW071832160426
43209CB00003B/279